Your Customer Service Matters:
5 simple steps to a great customer service company

Greg Saladino

This publication is designed to provide competent and reliable information regarding the subject matter covered. However, it is sold with the understanding that the author and publisher are not engaged in rendering legal, financial, or other professional advice. Laws and practices often vary from state to state, and if legal, financial, or other expert assistance is required, their services of a professional should be sought. The author and publisher specifically disclaim any liability that is incurred from the application or use of the contents in this book.

GS Books
8927 Hypoluxo Rd, Suite A145
Lake Worth, FL 33467

Copyright 2022 by Greg Saladino
All rights reserved. This book, or parts thereof, may not be reproduced in any form without written permission.

Printed in the United States of America

Library of Congress in Cataloging in Publication Data

Saladino, Greg
Your Customer Service Matters: 5 simple steps to a great customer service company

ISBN: 978-0-578-61839-5
LCCN:

Contents

About the author

Intro: The Keys to Customer Service

Chapter 1: Hire the right people   1-17

Chapter 2: Set the rules (Vision)   18-34

Chapter 3: Build the Culture   35-46

Chapter 4: Involving Everyone   47-57

Chapter 5: Continuously Train and develop   58-67

Chapter 6: Putting it all together   68-73

Bonus: Thoughts on work attitude   74-82

About the Author

I was born in New York and grew up between there and Florida. I was exposed early in life to business and customer service by my family who always taught me the possibilities are endless. I am thankful every day for the lessons that they taught me.

An Entrepreneur since the beginning; I started my first business in 5th grade selling candy and evolved into multiple people selling candy for me. Later while in college I started my first organized business selling beepers on campus. I provided a complete one stop order and delivery experience that customers loved. This developed into a full-service beeper and cell phone store within a few months. Through my superior customer service, I was able to build and sell the store to move into the corporate world. Starting in an entry level position with a Fortune 500 company, I moved up within the ranks in various sales, service, and management positions. I remain with the same company, moving through the ranks to multi-location management in the South Eastern territory.

From the beginning of my business endeavors, I always knew I must provide better service then my competition. At the start of my career, I didn't always know what this looked like, but I was always taught to treat everyone the same and with great care. I made sure at every step my team and I went the extra mile for our customers, and this has served me well through my career.

I was privileged to work for a great company and had many great mentors along the way. These mentors came not only from leadership I reported to but from coworkers and teammates that had the experience and knowledge to guide me.

As I moved through the ranks in corporate America, I realized that many people talk about customer service but fall short when it comes to execution. I was able to stand out as a great promoter of customer service which led me to want to share my thoughts on what customer service should be.

My goal and mission of this book is to bring the knowledge of great customer service to as many people as possible. This book is set up to help individuals and companies build and sustain great customer service.

Acknowledgements

I want to thank my family for supporting me in this project. You were with me every step of the way to make sure the second book was just as good as my first one.

Thank you for putting up with my 60-70-hour work week, travel and still pushing me to keep going on this book in my down time. COVID may have slowed this down but we still accomplished the goal.

I also want to thank my work family with whom I have grown up with for giving me the challenges and knowledge to pass on to others.

This book could not have happened without you!

Intro:

We are in a challenging time where things are changing quickly; technology is moving and speed matters. This natural progression of the business environment along with the COVID Pandemic has forever changed customer service and the way our customers want to be served. Businesses are looking to provide a great product or service with competition coming from areas no one would have imagined 5 years ago. Great customer service is necessary in every business to compete in this environment.   Does everyone have good service? No, some of them do not even realize it and that is their potential downfall.

Businesses that are not providing good customer service are in very real danger of being out of business within the next 10 years. With added transparency of online surveys, social media and instant access, the consumer has more power than ever to either build your business or bring it crumbling down.

Complicating this further is COVID which has challenged the way most companies do business in general let alone how they provide their customer service.

The question becomes, "is your company customer service friendly or is it just one of the many companies that will fail?" Which would you want? I think the answer is obvious.

This does not only encompass the business being a great customer service business, but it also requires that your employees are great customer service advocates. The question that comes up is, "are you a customer service friendly person or not?" Some people cannot be a customer service person, no matter what position they are currently in. They just have an attitude that does not allow them to serve customers. Many companies out there claim to provide great customer service but do not make sure their team perform at the same level of service that they promise. This causes a big difference in the leadership's perceived service they provide verses the actual service their people are providing

The companies that provide outstanding service will not only survive but they will thrive.

There are thousands of books about customer service. They explain what type of person needs to do customer service and what types of techniques to use but the only way you can truly provide customer service is if you genuinely care for your customers. With thousands of books out there, why is this book different?

This book is different in that the author has been in the customer service business for over 26 years and has seen the development of the new way we do business firsthand. I have seen the major shift between talking about customer service verses providing great service. Many companies have come and gone and only the strong customer-oriented companies will survive. Simply talking about good customer service no longer does the job.

Twenty years ago, customer service was just a thought in a business's plan. There were not really many companies out there trying to provide great customer service or forming a culture to do so. Revenue and profit were king. If you could provide good service, fine but if it was to sacrifice profit, no way. They didn't get that if you provide great service, you will get more revenue and more profit. It's a win for the customer and a win for the company.

The real focus must be the customer every time. The customer controls everything and in today's times they can voice their opinion instantly and can affect your business instantly. You must always be aware that the customer has more power than they have ever had over how your business appears.

Websites and phone apps such as Google reviews, Yelp, Home advisor, Nextdoor and others are giving consumers instant insight on how a company is treating its customers. These are things that companies must make sure they are aware of and must know how to react to and get great reviews. Great reviews tell people who to do business with. They are as important as a person-to-person referral in our time. In fact, they may even be more important, they are further reaching. In this book we will discuss what I feel are the keys to great customer service. Many things come into play when caring for your customers and it does not matter which type of business you are engaged in. Every business is a service business. It does not matter if you are selling a product or a service, your customers expect that you will meet their expectations and do it with a smile. Let me repeat that, every business is a service business.

No matter what you sell or service you provide it is a customer service business and you should act accordingly. You are not selling an item if you want repeat business you are selling your customers and potential future customers on why to use you and your business.

When I look at most of the companies out there, they do not provide the customer service that they should. They simply do not deliver on their promises and do not have systems to make sure great service happens.

We break this book down into five sections that I call the 5 keys to providing great customer service.

5 Keys to great customer service:

Hire the right people

Set the rules

Build the culture

Involve everyone

Continuously train and develop

We will discuss each of these and put it all together in simple terms that your team can understand and use daily. The goal of this book is to help you build a culture and continue to develop your customer service organization.

Communication is key in customer service and getting everyone involved is imperative to your success. It is ongoing and must be continuously monitored and talked up.

If you can build the culture you can not only survive in this environment, you and your company can thrive. You must provide great customer service at every step.

Chapter 1

Hire the right people

In our search to have a great customer service company the most important thing we can do is often the biggest and most overlooked one. We must hire the right people in every position that serves our customers from reception to the senior management. Everyone must be on board.
I say this is overlooked because we do not take enough care in hiring the best person in every position. We don't regard all positions as key positions. Most companies talk about hiring the best but when it comes down to it, they fail on many levels. Panic hiring sets in and we do not pick the right people for the job. In addition, we do not search at all levels to pick great people.

This is increasingly difficult since COVID as many people are making more staying home on unemployment than they were when they were working. This compounds the issue which we all hope is resolved soon. As of this writing it is still a major issue as we move towards herd immunity, a percentage of the population vaccinated, we can hope that we continue to free people up, so they are encouraged to get out and work. While we hope everything gets better, COVID and its variants will continue to plague our world most likely for at least the next few years. Even as everything normalizes, we must look at every position as the most important position to our company.

Most hiring managers tend to overlook many positions as unimportant, and this is a major failure. Business owners and operators normally look to hire people to do main jobs for the service or product they sell. They need to emphasize the same hiring practices for every position that services customers, both internal and external. There is no position in a company that is less important than another and at the end of the day every person within a company has contact with external, internal customers, or both.

As an example, let us use the car dealership. When they go to hire people for a car dealership, the ones they focus on are the salespeople and management team. They find the best salespeople that can close as many deals as possible.
The ideal candidate for them should be someone that can provide relationships and can impress your customers, not just close deals. Creating relationships with the customers is the only way the dealership will become successful. They must make sure they not only are able to sell cars, but they are able to wow the customers to ensure they have repeat business and referrals to ensure the business growth.

Once they make sure they have the best salespeople they can build the business they will need to have people to service the existing accounts.

They will then go find some of the best mechanics or service technicians and make sure that they are well trained to repair the vehicles. These people also should be able to advise customers of what they did and carry-on normal conversation to explain what they did. A lot of time the soft skills are overlooked. A mechanic, while usually working with computers and vehicles, still needs to be able to communicate with both his boss and in some instances the customers. In some dealerships you end up knowing the mechanics, and sometimes they do not. In the dealerships that are small they must communicate with the customers directly and must do so daily. If they do not handle this correctly you end up having very poor customer service.

The last thing that they will usually do is choose people to answer the phone and cashiers to check out customers. In this case, these people are probably some of the most important people you will end up hiring but these people are chosen because they know how to do tasks and answer a phone. They will not necessarily be the best person to deal with the customers. When this happens, there is a complete breakdown in the customer service experience. This could be a major issue and likely will be. Gone are the days when the clerk can brush off customers as a bother.

The front-line customer reps are the people that answer the phones and check out people when they receive their service. Again, these are lower paying positions, but they are very important to your business and if you overlook them your business will end up failing.

Let's go back to the salespeople they are hiring in this fictional auto dealership. When we are selecting them, what are we looking for in their abilities to sell? Are we looking for people to build relationships with the customers for long lasting business or do we just hire the smoothest talking person you can find? The second choice will get you a bunch of sales, but it might affect your customer service. The idea is to make your company consistent and truly a great customer service company and if you do not hire the right salespeople, you can jeopardize that. There is a fine line here on what you should do, and I always recommend looking at the personality and judging from there. Ask questions relating to how your candidate will deal with customer service issues by using a simulation to see how they would theoretically react.

A simulation would consist of an interview that has a customer service scenario that they have to handle. An example of this would be A customer comes in upset their car is not ready; walk me through what you would do. They must be able to give you a solution.

When you are hiring people in any industry, you must hire friendly people that like dealing with customers. If you do not hire people who love your customers, you will not be able to build a service culture in your business. So, what do you look for in that person? The first thing I would look for in a great customer service person is a smile... You cannot teach someone that does not like to smile and be happy to do that... The second thing that you must look for is a person that can take someone yelling at them or being upset and not take it personal. There are many people in our work force that will not be able to handle upset customers. Those type of people cannot work for your organization or you will never provide great customer service.

There are many ways to figure this out. As I stated above, one is a simulation to see how they react to a situation. When you do a simulation, you must have it laid out clear and really pay attention to how the applicant answers the questions. Do they become defensive, or do they keep that smile during the whole situation? You might want to also ask what situations that they helped a customer that was upset. Good stories are tough to make up on the spot and when they have details, you have a good chance they are telling the truth.

They must be able to keep composure in every situation. A customer service rep often is yelled at and they must be able to keep their composure no matter what happens. Often when they are yelled at or blamed for issues, they have no control of, and they need to be able to show empathy to the customer and not take it personal. When they relate to what they are talking about without getting defensive or taking it personal, they will end up solving the customer's problem and making them happy. Their job is to make sure the customer gets off the phone happy.

If the person you are hiring or have hired does not understand that their whole job is to satisfy customers than you need to keep looking. The selection process can be hard, but don't you want your customers to have the best experience? I know I do.

Remember, there is a certain mentality many employees have that you must get past. Many people in the workforce think they work too hard for the money that they earn. This is a very bad problem in today's society as people are not willing to put in the work to get the experience to make more money. Of course, this is perception, and you can influence this perception by taking care of your employees. You must provide an outstanding work environment to make sure your employees are happy that they are working with you.

There is a sense of entitlement that a lot of the employee pool has. This is a hard thing to get past and as employees in customer service we must build a certain level of pride in our employees. They are not only serving our customers but have the pride in knowing that if they do well, they will be rewarded for it.

How many times have you run across a poor customer service rep? I can think of many, from the phone to in person it is rampant in our world. Do you remember the last poor customer service experience you had? I do and I have told a bunch of people about it already. Many of your customers will do the same if they have a bad experience with someone that represents your company. How can you prevent it as an employer? You must hire the right people to start with.

Customers want to see happy people serving their needs, whether it's for fast food or buying a television they don't want to see miserable people. They do not want people to argue with them, the customer is always right is what is expected. To have a truly customer service-oriented company you must have happy people working for you. Happy people treat your customers right, and therefore, build your business.

They must want to serve your customer. In today's environment people are used to great service whether it is from Amazon or from Uber or from your company. Consumers expect the same level of service as these great customer service companies. If you cannot deliver that service, they will find someone else to fill their need. Are we spoiled by this great service and customer is always right attitude? I would say yes and therefore, you must hire the right people, or your vision and your company will not fulfill your customers' expectations. It's not a good idea to want to serve the customer, it is simply a requirement to do the job.

I will give you a good example of poor customer service that I experienced recently.

I called my cable provider recently with a question about my bill. I wasn't upset at this point; I just had a few questions and thought that I was being over charged.

I got a representative that was not very willing to help me and in fact she was unwilling to the point of sighing. She was simply unwilling to help and intent on making it difficult to do business with her and her company. I asked her, "did you just sigh at me"? Her answer was the most unbelievable response I could think of. I couldn't even make this up, she said to me, "I am in charge of my bodily functions." I asked her again and she repeated it. This really got me upset to the point my blood was boiling and I said to her, "So if you had to pass gas on the phone that would be ok?" She repeated it again and I said please let me talk to your supervisor, to which she replied ok.

Stopping there, she was willing to pass the phone to not have to deal with a customer that has a problem. It was very easy for her to pass me off because her manager obviously was ok with it. When this type of behavior is tolerated it will continue to breed a group of people who are ok with providing poor customer service.

Her manager then came on the phone about 5 minutes later and said, "what is your problem with my rep?" I explained what happened, and she then said, well she is responsible for her own bodily functions.

What the heck is wrong with this company, I thought? Apparently so much that they were the star of a YouTube video entitled "XXXXX does not give a F**k!" I then asked for the corporate number for the president of the company. They would not give me the number, so I up hung up and I researched the phone number on the internet. I found the President of Florida and called him. His office did call me and did eventually fix the problem, but I will never forget that experience and have told that story hundreds if not thousands of times.

Did I need to go through all of that to fix my issue? Heck no, it was very easily solved and probably wouldn't have cost them anything at the start and ended up with them giving me about 4 months of free service. It was a stupid interaction and gave me a bad taste about that company for a lifetime.

The sad thing about the whole experience is that they are probably the best out there that does what they do. The issue is they are not watching their customer service reps. They most likely have the best tech people, best development, and research but they lack the basic positions that make a company outstanding.

This type of poor service leads to loss of market share and new opportunity for new companies to start up and fill the gap at best. At worse this can lead to a company, no matter how big, to go out of business.

I have so many stories about bad customer service that I can probably fill up a whole book with poor customer service stories. That would be a depressing book for me and for all the companies that I would have to mention. These companies are known in my mind for poor customer service, yet they might just be a victim of poor hiring.

What could they have done to prevent this? The main thing is to make sure they hired the correct people for the position. You cannot hire a person that does not want to help people to handle your customer service. This is something I have seen repeatedly.

The two people I talked to should be nowhere near customers and should not be interacting with them, at all. Is this company a bad company? Not really because if they were, they would not have solved my problem when I got to the president of the company. Do they have bad team members working for them, absolutely?

The next thing I want to explore is the team members who do not encounter external customers. These team members deal mostly with internal customers (other team members) and are often also overlooked regarding customer service. Anyone in corporate America knows who these people are, these are the ones that you dread calling when you need help. So why does it matter if a team member that only talks to employees has poor customer service, how much damage can they do?

In my opinion, these team members can cause as much issue in an origination as the person handling the external customers. Let me give you an example of an issue I had recently.

A team member had a mistake on his paycheck regarding child support. Additional money was taken out and it needed to be corrected. He called the payroll department and explained the situation, they told him to follow up next week, so they have time to figure out what happened. He called the next week and spoke to the same person and was surprised when the person he called acted like they had no clue what he was taking about. Not only that, but when he asked don't you remember, we spoke about this last Tuesday; she replied, "do you know how many people I speak with, how would I remember your issue?"

Two things happened here; one she showed a lack of concern for the customer (our employee) and two she basically said his issue didn't matter to her. He did end up escalating this to me and we got it resolved but the moral to a front-line employee was damaged and, in some cases, especially if this causes a hardship, we could have a disgruntled team member serving our customers. Worse than that we can end up losing a great employee because of the indifference or poor customer service of another. This is a big problem that happens in many corporations, it's very widespread and companies need to take notice and fix it. It has very serious repercussions that in many cases cannot be quantified. If you think this doesn't happen in your organization, you are not looking hard enough.

A lot of the time these types of issues go unnoticed by management as they are not reported to the supervisor. This is and ends up being a major issue and you must figure out how to solicit this information, so the problem doesn't grow. It could be the person you least expect doing these types of things, possibly someone who has been there for many years. You must flush these people out of your organization, or you can damage or possibly lose your business.

Therefore, when hiring a new person, you must have a simulation that is in line with the position you are hiring for. With a simulation you can pick up how the new candidate will deal with situations.

Once they have done a simulation and get past that there are some additional steps you should take. The next thing you want to do is make sure they do ride along or sit along with someone doing the job you are trying to fill. This is one of the most important things you can do, as they will give your employee more info than they will give you. The ride along should be with a trusted employee and they should know that you will want a recap of the ride along.

I have seen ride-a-longs that the prospective employee tells the employee that they are riding with, some crazy stuff, that they would never say in an interview. They will tell someone they think of as a coworker a lot more than they are going to tell you. If you can catch issues and cut them off at that point, you will save a lot of time and money and most likely a lot of customers that would not have been happy with his/her service.

So, let's recap, you must properly vet your potential hires and you must hire every position in the same way. You cannot deem any position as less or unimportant. Anyone that interacts with your external or internal customers' needs to be hired with care.

Hire the right people and you will be on your way to creating a great customer service culture. I would say this is the most important step you will take to becoming a truly great customer service company.

Chapter 2
Set the rules/vision

Once you have the right people in place to fulfil the customers' expectations you must figure out what your direction and vision will be. Do you want to be able to satisfy every customer you have? Are you making sure your internal customers are also being cared for? Do you want to impress them with how well your team caters to them? To get this done you must have a vision for what you want your customer service to be. As I said in the intro, I have been in the customer service business for over 25 years, and I have seen things change rapidly in business and customer service.

I was not always a believer in true customer service. I had it in me, but I did not quite know what it meant. I did not know how important it was, but it did come naturally. You must want to fix problems and be willing to do anything to make sure your customer is happy. Let me repeat that, to do well with customer service you must want to fix problems! You must want to help people and provide great customer service. Many people are in business or in a job to get paid and they lose sight of what their job really is.

To help your employees, provide the best customer service you must have vision. If you don't have a vision of what you want to happen there will be no way to possibly achieve your goals.

In setting your goals you need to be bold and really go after major goals such as "no unhappy customers" and you must mean it. This should not just be words and they must embody everything your company symbolizes. Everything you do must empower your team and organization to get it done.

One of my first lessons came very early in my career. As a new assistant manager in charge of service, I was calling on people that owed us money and came across an unhappy customer. Let's call him, Mr. N. I called him and he immediately started yelling at me that he did not owe any money and told me he never wants to see us again. He said he pays his bills, and he did not get the service as promised and wants his service cancelled now. I refused to let him cancel and told him I would be out there in 20 min. He told me, "don't come out here, I am not interested!" I kept on and finally convinced him. When I got out there, he was the nicest guy, and I serviced his house for free that day. He was so impressed with my response he continued his service and not only stayed with us, but he remained a customer until he passed away. He would call me when he had any issue and sometimes just to say hi. I not only kept the customer I made a friend out of the situation.

I have many stories about this customer, he always made me laugh and I always made sure his home was taken care of. Although the tech did take care of his home monthly, anytime he needed anything extra I was there to help. I didn't realize it at the time, but I think at that point, I learned to do whatever it takes to make people happy, no matter what. Do extra, go the extra mile and things will work out. Your customers will love you and stay for a long time. It is very simple, but you must want to do it. You must want to serve people and make them happy.

I have many stories like this and if you are truly providing great service you should too. Great service stories happen often when you expect and promote great service.

I tell that story because at that time I can tell you I did not really believe in customer service; I just wanted to save him and get the money he owed. Fortunately for me, it came naturally. Again, at that point I did not even know what customer service was. I knew as a business we were supposed to take care of our customers, but I still did not "get it". Many of your team are probably the same, they have no clue why they need to save customers.

As I stated previously true customer service happens because you want it to happen, its not a mistake, its not by chance. It's set up to happen and it is required.

In today's business environment, you had better believe in providing the best customer service possible. It is even more important than ever to have a "satisfy everyone attitude". You must be willing to do whatever it takes plus a little extra to make a customer happy. This must be part of the vision.

Business is more transparent, and you must react quickly to customer issues and provide superior customer service if you want to be the provider of choice. With today's technology if you provide poor customer service your customer can tell thousands of people with one tweet or post on social media.

The Story of Mr. N is a great story and I loved that I was able to satisfy him and his concerns. My company's policy and vision gave me the tools to be able to satisfy him. When we set a culture in the company, we must make sure that it is in line with our vision. I recently had a very poor customer service experience while finishing a lease on a vehicle.

I wanted to turn in my lease early on a vehicle from an Asian market upscale vehicle and I made several calls asking what I would have to do so I could figure out how much it was going to cost me to end the lease early.

To make a long story short I got the information and paid the last 3 months all at once and turned the car in. I also did the pre check that makes sure there aren't any additional charges to be associated with the turn in. About 2 months later I received a bill in the mail for a very trivial amount of money. I complained because no one ever told me about this fee in the calls that I made to the company. I was told there would not be any additional fees. The person on the phone said they agreed it doesn't make sense to lose a customer for $163.00, but they cannot do anything about it. So, at that point, they agreed that they didn't want to lose a customer for $163.00, but they did not have the tools to save me and waive the $163.00.

The only thing they would do was direct me to the contract and I was then told that there is nothing they can do. I must pay the $163.00. I paid it right then, but then I wrote to the executives of the company and posted my complaint in several social media outlets. I let everyone know that this business doesn't value their customers and relies on nickel and diming them. I have about 3000 total social media followings without LinkedIn, so plenty of people saw my complaint. After about a month, I received notice from the executive level saying the charge will not be refunded. By the time I received their response, I had already forgotten about it, but then their response was a further insult as far as I was concerned.

I will never buy a car from this company again so they lost the potential of 100's of thousands of dollars in new vehicle sales and finance costs because they couldn't refund $163.00 for a customer that was unhappy. To make matters worse 5 months later a derogatory remark was placed on my credit report. I monitor my credit so when I saw this, I had to make another call to the so called "luxury brand" to have it removed. They had it removed within a few weeks, but the point was I had to call once again and be bothered by something that should never have happened.

Let's think about that for a minute. I buy a new car every 24 to 36 months. Do the math, I'm 42 years old so I will most likely buy another 11 cars in my lifetime for my partner. At an average price of about $75,000 and an average loan/ lease charge for the finance company of $5,000. They have missed out on a potential $880,000 in sales/revenue and finance profits from refusing to give me a refund on $163.00.

In this case, not only a clerk, but the supervisor and the executive team is so unfocused on customer service that they would fight with a customer over $163.00. It is clear to me that this company is not customer focused and eventually this will become an issue for them. Do they make good cars? Yes, maybe great, but it doesn't matter if their service sucks.

What could the company have done differently? For one, they could have empathized with me and listened to what I was saying. I had everything documented as far as who I spoke with and what was said. It was clear that I did my homework and made sure I would not have any additional charges, yet still got charged. They could have had something in place to allow the people handling the customers to waive fees or at least reduce them.

To go all the way to executive level and still not have a solution that was ok just means the company is not focused on the customer and simply wants to sell cars and not build customer loyalty.

How many decisions do businesses make like this daily? Is your direction and vision set up to combat this? With social media people can post this info and it is permanent and will negatively affect your business.

I must repeat this, everything is out there for all to see and it is permanent. In addition to social media, there are review sites and blogs that people who have a huge audience can promote your company or send them to bankruptcy.

That was a bad story for that company, and they have already lost one opportunity since the issue happened to sell me a vehicle, we simply will not buy that brand.

Now let me give you a good story from a small company. The company is a local Vehicle Wrap company that specializes in Tint and PPF vehicle protection wraps. Recently I scraped the mirror on one of my vehicles and it damaged the wrap that was installed on the car. I texted this company that did the wrap before I bought it and the owner immediately responded. I told him the situation and he set up an appointment two days later. I went in, he put the new wrap on the mirror within 30 minutes. I asked him how much and he said, "Nothing, you are all set." I tried to pay him and even just tried to buy him, and his guy lunch, but he wouldn't take the money. I told him I would refer him, and I definitely will. He did not have to do that, but he is building his business around customer service and things like that show. He spent 30 minutes and probably $20.00 on material, but he left a lasting impression on me, the customer. In addition, thinking about it he could have charged me $150.00, and I would have paid and been happy.

He certainly is not in the financial position a large automaker is, but he focused on the customer and made me a customer for life. I will guarantee you the next car I buy will have PPF installed by him.

Great service will get you customers, but you must want to help people.

Let's talk a little bit about Facebook, Twitter, and Instagram. If I am upset with a company, I will post on my social media accounts and let everyone know who upset me. Many people do this every day and as a person who manages a customer service business you must be very aware of this. People are much more likely to put a bad review online that a good review.

As many of us do, we can immediately go on these platforms and share our bad experiences. Is this fair? Maybe not, but it is reality. The question is what can you do about these bad reviews? The first thing you must do is manage your vision and make sure your employees are all aware of your vision. Without letting everyone know what you expect you will not get the results you want.

The warning here is if you do not sell your vision to your team you will probably not succeed. In turn if you are not willing to really enhance your customer service experience in today's climate you will cease to exist over the next 10 years as a company.

People want service their way, in their time immediately in today's business climate. They will not accept excuses and they will not accept poor service. In fact, as stated above if you give them poor service, they are highly likely to go on Facebook, Twitter, Google, Yelp, Instagram, or any other new platform that comes out and complain about your service.

Like the adage goes, if you make a customer upset, they will tell 10 people, but if you make them happy, they might tell one person. The issue now is that there are so many users that with one touch of the keyboard, 10,000 people know about a poor service experience with your company. If you do not think that matters, you will learn very quickly that social media can make or break you in this new climate. One or two customers can quickly add up to thousands that have a poor perception of your company or service. This is not really where you want to be, and you can leverage this by providing great customer service to begin with.

You must be highly engaged in all social media platforms and really get the word out as to how good your services are. They must know your vision as well as your employees.

Some of the ways you can do that on the platforms is to ask for a good review. Most rating platforms frown upon asking for surveys from your existing customers because they feel you can manipulate the survey, by asking. I do not agree with that statement because to get people to talk about good services sometimes you do have to ask them. People are more likely to complain about a service done then to promote or tell people about a service that they received that was exceptional.

Therefore, I believe we must ask for reviews as a business and if we fail to do this, we will see our business slowly diminish. You might think I am trying to make you paranoid or sounding the alarm bells, which, in fact, I am. I see this very clearly in my business. Without a vision and plan you will not survive.

When you set the expectation or vision with your customer service people or your entire team, you must set clear concise expectations of what they should achieve. What does that mean to you? Set the rules very clearly and make the goals measurable.

I will give you an example; if you tell a group of people that you want to improve your canceled customers by 20% you most likely will never get to your number. If you take, the same goal and say you are currently cancelling 100 customers a month, you should reward that goal to tell your team that they cannot cancel more than 80 customers per month. That clear goal takes no math and is very easy for any employee on your team to understand.

The first goal with a percentage amount will be confusing for some and surprisingly they will not be able to calculate it. They might also have no idea how many cancels we have now. The other thing that you must do is you must break it down to the individual. Therefore, if you have 10 people that are responsible for cancels and your goal is 80 cancels or less each person can only have eight cancels. That goal must be very clear to each individual. Breaking it down this way, everyone will be responsible for that number and will be able to work towards it. This will also address how you will get your goals across to the whole team.

So, what is your vision for the company or business unit that you are responsible for? Do you have clear goals for your team? If you do not, how do you expect to achieve goals you do not have?

I have learned a lot from mentors through my life and career about goal setting and follow up. The first thing you must do as I alluded to above is set the goal. I use these five steps:

1. Set the goal.
2. Inform and sell the goal to everyone in the organization.
3. Divide the goal to the individuals.
4. Set a way to consistently measure.
5. Follow-up (relentlessly) and keep everyone informed.

If you follow these steps, you will most likely achieve your goal. The last one is the most important. Too many times, in my career, I have seen goals come and go... slogans and wasted programs. Without follow up, goals and vision mean nothing.

The next question is how do you set a customer service goal? What are you trying to achieve?

Once you know, what you are trying to fix or achieve you must set your goal and inform everyone. How are you going to do that? Meetings, emails, signs? Pick the plan, this is like a marketing plan, you are selling the goal. Do everything you can to make sure your team is on board.

Next you divide the goal into individual achievement. What does each team member have to do to get you to achieve your goal? After you establish this, you set up you're tracking. Tracking can be an excel form or any other type of tracking system that helps you track individuals and get you closer to your goal. These goals must be tracked per individual and department. We will talk more about this when we discuss getting everyone involved and follow up in a later chapter.

You must also have clear expectations on how to react to these reviews. Over the past year one of my goals was to improve the customer survey scores over my offices. I made it mandatory that any poor survey that comes in gets a visit from a manager within 24 hours. This was a clear direction to what I want the reaction to a bad customer experience to be. Everything stops, and you go out, now, to speak to our customer and see what happened. This has created a huge sense of urgency on my team's part. In addition, this is a "wow" for the customer. We have probably saved close to a hundred customers by doing this. I have gone out on some of these, and I have seen the reaction and surprise from the customers that not only did we read and see the survey, but we showed up the same day to solve the issue.

This is just one example of things you can do to create a vision and direction of a customer first experience.

You must declare the vision and make sure all your team knows what it is. Your vision of customer first is very important and you must project it to your team and your customers both old and new.

Chapter 3
Build the culture

We have all probably heard someone in our company or in another company say we need a Culture change. That is kind of a catch phrase in the corporate world. I remember the first time I ever heard the phrase, and I must tell you I was annoyed as a leader in my individual office. The culture in my office was great and I certainly didn't think that the corporate people were going to come change it for the better. In my mind it meant that for some reason, our leadership thought we had a poor culture.

As with many phrases used in corporate America it is misunderstood and many times not used correctly. A culture change usually means the culture is not good and needs to be changed, but for the most part it is not the company, it is the leaders who are the issue.

As I stated above, the company I work for is a wonderful company with an outstanding culture, yet I have heard the phrase culture change many times through my career. And time and time again when I heard it, I questioned what we were trying to change.

Our culture is clear if you read our manuals, we strive to provide excellent service, period. Our leaders have also shown the same interest and concern in customer service. So why would we change the culture? What we really needed to change in some areas were the leaders in the individual offices or regions. In a lot of cases that is exactly what happened.

The question we need to ask is who determines what kind of service you provide, the company or the people? If you thought people, you are correct.

People, your team, determine what kind of service is provided. These people or your team will do what you guide them to do, your leadership counts. If you are a manager or an owner, you are responsible for your team or company and you will determine if you allow your team to fail or become successful. I firmly believe no one comes to work to fail, they just do not focus. Think of your worse team member right now...do you think he or she comes to work to fail, that they wake up on Monday and say, "wow it's Monday, I'm going to try to do a shitty job today". That just doesn't happen. Do people do a shitty job? Heck yeah... but they do not intend to.

Many factors cause them to do a poor job and it is your job to determine what is going wrong and how can you fix it. Sometimes, unfortunately, you cannot fix it. They may not be in the correct job. Sometimes they do not know the vision, or they are not being motivated in their job. The second and third reason could be our fault as leaders. This is the first step in affecting the culture. You as a leader must get your vision to your people in the front lines and that is the hard part. Especially if you oversee multiple locations, it is sometimes hard to get your vision to your front-line team members.

The good news is with technology it is not as hard as it was 5 years ago. With today's technology we have email, text, YouTube, Group Me, Teams, Zoom and many other platforms you can use to communicate directly to the team in real time. We already discussed creating the vision which is the first step to building the culture. The second thing you must do is repeat your vision until everyone on the team can recite your vision or at least know what your main objective is.

An example of this would be if your vision were to have the best customer service in your Industry. If one of your team members is asked what the main goal is, they should be able to repeat that without thinking. When you get your team to do that you are on your way to instilling a customer service culture.

The team must know your vision very clearly or you will not get the traction you need to build your business into a real customer service powerhouse. You don't want to just have a message that they can repeat, you want them to live customer service. You must make sure your team is impowered and ready to act to elevate your customer service at every step of the customer service experience.
A few years ago, I was talking to one of the leaders in the company I work for about Chick-fil-a and how all their employees say "my pleasure" after every interaction. He was saying something that stuck with me the last few years that I now share his same thought process. I don't know if he would remember the conversation, but it revolved around these thoughts. When someone says thank you many people say, "No problem". You have heard it before; you may have even said it before. I am here to tell you now, "No problem" in response to thank you is unacceptable. Why would them doing something to help a customer be a problem?

We do not think about it but that is just crazy. Your words matter and you must act accordingly. As you can probably guess I have plenty of stories of poor service and I also have one regarding "No problem".

I called for take out from a chain restaurant that serves steak and other meals with an Australian flavor. They do a great job, and my local restaurant is usually on their game and this was the first time I had an issue with their food or their service.

I ordered a few steaks and when I got home one of the steaks were not good. I don't like to complain but it was inedible.

When I called to complain they said they would take care of it and they gave the call to the manager. When he got on the phone he apologized and he said, "Just bring it back, no problem..." I immediately got a bit annoyed as it was a problem and by him saying "no problem", he diminished my complaint because it was a problem as now instead of eating, I was driving back to the restaurant.

I probably got a bit hostel with him on the phone and said, "I want to speak to you when I get there".

When I got there, he was there, he explained his no problem comment, and I told him why that made me annoyed and how it really did not show empathy and diminished my complaint. We had a 15-minute conversation about customer service; He thanked me and said he appreciated what I corrected him on, and that he never looked at it that way. He also told me this was his first store, and he would share this feedback with his team in the hopes they would handle things like this better.

I have taught this to my team, and I expect that they use that attitude when helping any customer ... why would helping them be a problem? It would not be, right? So, what you say and how you say it matters. So, replace "no problem" with "my pleasure". It will work, I promise.

So how else can you change the culture? Make a big deal when a customer has an issue. To truly provide great service you must make a big deal about issues your customers have and you must take quick action. Customers do not have to use our service; they have many choices. Do not give them a reason to use someone else.

If a customer has an issue, as a leader, you must ask questions, many questions. You must make sure your team knows you will ask so many questions, which will make them really try to solve the issue and make customers happy. Everyone working for you must know you will only accept exceptional service from him or her.

When a customer calls in to complain 99.9% of the time, we gave them a reason to complain. There are very few people in our world that will take the time to call you and complain if we did everything right. When I think about it, I cannot remember one time in my career that a customer called just to complain without us doing anything to cause the issue. Not one time, it simply does not happen often; people don't have time.

Let us give some examples of how we can help with customer issues. A lot of the time it is just communication.

Mrs. Rodriguez calls and tells your customer care person; I want to cancel my service. What is the person that answers response? Do we say ok? What should we say? Why are you firing us? Do we empathize with the issue they have? Do we offer a solution? It does not matter what business you are in, if you do not ask questions, you will not solve the customer's issue. Are they having an issue with your product or service? These are questions you must get answers on. Keep asking questions until you get to the root of the problem, then offer a solution. Solve their problem! It's not magic.

How would you solve this cancelation issue? Would you ask the questions or just let Mrs. Rodriguez cancel? Most of the time the call is for help, help to solve an issue that they have. Companies are judged not if they make a mistake but what they are willing to do to fix the mistake and make sure it doesn't happen again. Most people just want the problem solved and if they get it solved, they will be happy. The issue that usually comes in is that the person on the phone does not ask the correct questions or they inflame the customer more by acting indifferent to their issue. The customer must be able to have their problem or issue solved the first time without complicating matters more.

Solving the problem with one call requires one main thing and that is giving up control. What do I mean by giving up control? I mean empowering your people. Empower your people to take care of the issues without you or other supervisors getting upset about how they handled the issue. This is easier said than done. The challenge that always comes up is how much can you offer and what are you willing to do to save customers. There needs to be parameters, but you cannot get mad when people deviate from them in the name of satisfying a customer. Furthermore, they must know that you are willing to save customers, no matter what. Keeping the ones, you have is much better and a more economical strategy then letting them go to sell new ones. This is where what we talked about earlier regarding every position being important, not just certain positions that are usually considered key.

Customers want to handle an issue with one call. Make it easy for them and they will continue to use your business.

Here is another example of how to do the right thing that wins and keeps customers.

Mr. Jones calls in and he says that your salesperson was at the house and proposed a job. He says they did not offer any payment options and he saw on TV that the company offers them.

What do you do in the situation? You should empathize right away and make sure you understand why the customer is upset and start stating some solutions quickly. Once you have this issue solved with the customer you must ask yourself, Did the salesperson provide good customer service? I think not, he did not offer the customer options and that is bad customer service. As I stated above you must address this quickly with solutions but what does the person on the phone do with that call? Do they help, pass it back to the salesperson that messed up in the first place, or get the manager involved? I would say all the above. Of course, it would depend on what the policies are in your specific company, but it would be great for the person answering the phone to be able to help this customer.

In addition, what does the manager do once he gets involved? He/she should address this issue and make sure it doesn't happen again. If you do not expect your manager to get involved, you are not truly committed to great customer service. If the manager or owner doesn't get involved in these issues, they are not really customer service focused.

Getting everyone involved is exceptional customer service and it does not have to be the actual product or service can also be on the sales and support end of it. You must build the culture.

The culture that you need to build is the customer service culture and the only way to do that is to set the vision of being the best; Truly providing outstanding service to your customers.

The culture that you build is the foundation that will build your people up to perform the best possible customer service. To truly have a customer service culture in any business you must get everyone involved and you must have the correct people.

Chapter 4
Getting the team involved

In the last chapter we mentioned to be successful you must get everyone involved in everything you do. This means everyone from the janitor to the CEO; everyone needs to be on the same page. This seems like this would be an obvious statement, but too many times companies fail to get their vision down to the front lines. The vision is not explained correctly to the team and therefore they fail.

Once your whole team is involved with the problem or situation you will accomplish your goals. I have found no matter what the goal is, if you work on it and track it you will achieve it.

So how do you get everyone involved and make sure that everyone cares about the success of the company? The first thing that must happen to get your team involved and all working towards the same goal is to make it worth it for them.

Everyone wants to know what is in it for him or her no matter how good of a team member they are, and everyone should benefit from making the goals.

Sometimes the benefit isn't monetary, it might be recognition.

In the past, I have heard people say well it is their job so they should do it anyway. It is correct that it is their job, but human nature just does not work that way. They need and want incentive to go the extra mile.

So, what do you do to get your team involved? There are many different strategies to get your team involved. First, do you know that you have the right team in place? Going back to the last few chapters some people will never get fully involved because they just want to make a paycheck.

That goes back to our second chapter in the importance of finding the right people for each position. Once you have the right people for each position how you motivate them to do their best and provide exceptional service for your company and for the team. This is a constant, you must continue to recruit and find new talent. The person that was great for your company 5 years ago might not be the right fit now. I'm not saying that they do not have a place or cannot be retrained, but they must be a willing participant to the company's goals. If they are not it is time to move on and chose different people for those positions.

You must find out what, individually, drives each member of your team. People are driven by many different things; recognition, some people are driven by being liked by others, some people want more free time and other people are driven by money.

Typically, the people that are providing service in your company are driven more by recognition and being liked. They want the recognition and praise; they live to serve. They want and thrive on their customers wanting to do business with them. Then you have your sales departments, and they are usually driven by money, which is why they are in sales. They better be driven by money or you will have a very weak sales force. They still love the at-a-boys/girls, but they really want money and that is why they are in sales. A $20.00 gift card can go a long way for a salesperson, they want that money.

Everyone is going to be different. Some of the people in sales are going to be more motivated by just the thrill of the kill, then the money. Some service people are going to be motivated by making as much money as possible versus being liked by others that is where you must get to know your team.

The first step of getting any team where you want them to be is to get to know them. You must get close to your direct team and get to know them as much as possible. This is key to attaining your goals. This will teach you what drives them. Do they love vacations, do they love boating, and do they want to buy a home? What drives them to come to work every day and want to do their best what do they want to achieve?

This requires your attention and dedication to people which is the only way you can have great customer service. Think about your team right now, do you know them? You are not going to know everything about them, but you should know them enough to read what they want and what drives them. If you run multi-unit businesses, you must also instill this in your direct management reports. They must know their team.

Once you know that you will be able to model your incentives and conversation around what they like and what their hopes and dreams are.

Knowing your team is essential but your team knowing you is also something that is necessary for your team to thrive.

Getting to know them also involves treating them correctly and listening to them. There are far too many companies that do not listen to employees. This is also something that is overlooked by a lot of leaders they do not let their team get to know them. I don't know what the issue or fear that some leaders have with this, but it is something I see all the time. There is a fine line between what you tell your team and let them know about your life vs what you do not. There are certain things that are personal, and you might not want to share. You must be human to your team for them to follow you willingly. You also must instill confidence that you know what you are doing, you are successful, and you can help them become successful.

At this point, if you really know your team, you will be able to keep them involved in every step of the way. It is very important to make sure that you constantly over communicate with each department in your team. Yes, over communicate… What I mean by over communicating is you must have meetings and sessions with your team to keep everybody apprised of any new situations and what the daily activities involve. The easiest way to lose your team is when things change, you do not involve everybody, and you do not make sure that they are aware of the changes. No one on your team will appreciate changes happening without being told by you.

With COVID this has been very hard to do, but it can be done. When your team becomes disconnected from you and the rest of the team, things can go bad quickly.

This is a tough part about leading a team. Everyone gets busy in their own little world and it is very difficult to keep everybody apprised of the situation.

Things happen quickly in business, so as those changes are made, you really need to schedule meetings to make sure that you keep everybody up to date at least on a weekly basis. It is also important to bring the team together at least monthly as a group, to make sure you can inform them of the wins and losses.

If the team does not know if they are winning or losing, there is no way to get the best out of them. This is essentially like playing a football game and not having a scoreboard, nobody knows what is going on, nobody knows if you're winning or losing, and people generally get bored and quit the game.

The last thing you want your team to do is "quit the game". This is where we all lose big.

Moving even past just checking in your team, Monthly performance appraisals is also another way to make sure that your team is involved. If your team does not know, individually, where they stand it is very difficult for them to know what they must correct and what they are doing well. This will make a team fail, as they can create their own narrative, which can destroy the team quickly. If this is happening, in your operation, you must pull everyone together quickly and get the connectivity back in your business. This is key to great customer service.

Throughout the years, I have come across many people who think they are doing a good job but are simply not having the numbers or performance that they expect. Most of the time this happens due to a manager or supervisor not wanting to confront the employee. With the employee taking this as their performance as good enough. Mediocrity is a major killer for any service business. This is where everyone needs to be involved, coached, and appraised, frequently.

You must set high standards and we must be able to articulate those standards to her/his team and make sure that, if they are not at our standards, that they are coached up to be at our standards.

Not evaluating people on a consistent basis and holding them accountable also can breed dissention when you start holding them accountable. If you have a team member who hasn't been held accountable and you suddenly start holding them accountable you will most likely have an issue.

Recently I had an example of this. I had a team member who was a good person but was put into a position that they should not have been elevated to. They were also a 20-year employee that had never been documented as far as I could find and had a bit of a sense of entitlement. In situations like this it becomes clear that there is more work to be done on how you hold them accountable. The first documentation I gave him was a plan of action. This was received ok, and he said he understood what was needed. The next month I had to document him for not doing what I wanted him to do. Now there was a lot of unhappiness in the conversation because after 20 years of employment, 5 of that working for me, he was getting written up for the first time. So, in his eyes, who is the bad guy? Now I have a disgruntled team member who is being held accountable but might be disengaged at this point because no one ever held him to a higher standard.

Unfortunately, this did not work out and we ended up separating ways after a few months of things not getting done. This was a clear case of not holding someone accountable working against them and the business.

As I showed in the example, they will not understand why they are now being held accountable and could possibly not comply with what you are trying to enforce. This is because they were never held accountable and now you are trying to hold them accountable for their service or performance. This has happened to me several times when I took over an operation and there were under performers that were not documented or told that they need to step it up. The example stated was just one of many. It is very important to set the stage early and make sure everyone knows the expectations.

Once you are consistently communicating with your team, there is no way you will lose. Your team will become stronger, your numbers will become bigger, and you will be able to achieve any of the goals that you put forth. When you have a team that is working together, knows where they are and is communicating on a regular basis you will always win.

Let's recap what we have so far. We have a few more things left to discuss but let's list what we have so far.

1. Hire the right people for each job.
2. Set the vision so that everyone understands.
3. Build the culture around that vision.
4. Get everyone involved.

This is the start of the blueprint to customer service success. We are not done yet though; we need to tighten it up and make sure we continue to work on our skills.

Chapter 5
Training and development

One of the most important things you can do for your team is consistently and constantly train them. If you are not doing this and spending the time with them in the front lines you will not have a great service company.

You must ask yourself, "How do you train your new team members?" Is the training good or just a box to check? If you really want to be successful you need to look at your entire training, policies, procedures and, if applicable, your training department. Training is the most important part of your new team members onboarding. When you get a new team member, you must train them and keep them engaged from the very beginning. This is not optional, and they must be onboarded correctly, or you can ruin your chances of having a great team member.

It is also very important that any new team member is introduced to everyone on the team immediately. Everyone needs to know the new team member and the team member needs to know the rest of the team. This will foster good communication from the start. This will also weed out any issues you might have with a new team member. We must make sure they are a fit for the team, and this will be clear, very quickly, if there is good communication.

The first day a new team member is brought on board should feel very special to them. They are making a change in their life that hopefully becomes a long-term career for them. They are nervous and they do not know what to expect. This is when we can "wow" them and invite them to the team. They must feel that they are important and that they are not just a cog in a big wheel but that they are very important to the operation. You hired them because you saw something in them that told you they would be successful. Let them know and feel that. The first day you should be spending your time with them and making sure they are welcome. Take them to lunch and make it a special day. This is a very important part of getting to know your team and making sure new team members know you and trust that you will support them to achieving their goals.

Your training system should require your new team members to work with your other team members, but also have the time to work on their own. What I mean by that is, after the initial training you must make sure that they get to have time to train doing the job they will do, on their own, without supervision.

For example, if you have someone that is going to be on the phone, they need to be able to train with someone that is already on the phone helping customers. Part of that training must involve them taking the calls and being supervised by a veteran customer care agent. This will provide them the real-world experience and give them real-time feedback from someone that knows what they are doing.

You also, as their supervisor, need to be able to follow up and make sure that the training schedule is going as planned. If you do not do this part, you can very quickly have a disgruntled team member that does not feel like the training that you promised them is adequate.

This is real life simulation. When you or your coworker is training this person, you must be able to pick out issues and correct them at the beginning. Also, you must deliver on your promise of proper training.

I have had this experience before. My most recent experience with this was when we made a change to our training department. The training department, in the middle of one of my managers training, changed the entire platform of the management-training program. This change was not communicated properly, and, as managers, we were not trained in the program. This provided a gap that made some trainees very uncomfortable and confused.

If I were not communicating with my trainees, I would have never known this. I had a few trainees that were very uncomfortable and getting upset, with the training, as it was not going according to schedule. These types of things must be limited and the only way to limit these things is to communicate with your teams. I was able to jump in and fix it because I was involved in their training, but I can tell you that the other people in my position did not do regular reviews and were not caught up with the system as I was. Again, the company I work for is a top training company not only in the industry but of all companies and yet we still had this issue.

Even if the plan is great, it still must be executed with great care and relentless follow up.

The training for your team members should also include training in positions outside their main job duties. All team members should be cross training in as many jobs as possible.

In our current job climate as of this writing there is a shortage of workers and it is in your best interest to hire people that are multi-faceted and can learn new things. By doing this you have a much stronger work force. One thing that served me well in my career and life is having to work from the base positions in our company. I started in service and then went over to sales, then into management. This was not done in the traditional training program; I was doing the jobs, but it is a good idea to make sure that your training program allows your team to see and spend time with your team in all different positions before they head out to serve your customers. This is more important in jobs where your team members have more autonomy such as service technicians, outside salespeople, and other mobile positions. They must be able to relate to the other people on the team.

Your training program should allow for field ride-a-longs or in an inhouse position in house time with other positions including administration and phone customer service people. Each team member needs to understand what the other team member does and accomplishes daily. This brings team unity and ensures that each team member knows the importance of the other team member's job.

Remember a new employee or team member coming to work for you is putting a lot of faith in your company and most of the time in you. They put faith in you and trust they will be able to have a successful career and take care of themselves and/or their family. It is very important to them to make sure that the new career works out. Make sure you support them every step of the way. Your main goal should be to make them happy with their decision to come work with you.

If you are reading this book for your own company and you feel the need to revise your entire training program, it must be in tune with both your vision and the needs of your new trainees. Whether it be a person providing service to customers in person, or helping customers on the phone, you must make sure that you are fulfilling all your new employees training needs. Everything you train them on must follow your vision and culture.

If you do not communicate with them, you will not know that there is an issue, you could lose a good team member. You could even lose several team members. If you can execute the training, correctly, you can make a lot of money and provide great service for your customers.

Once you have them initially trained, does the training stop? The answer is, training should never stop, and training must be continuous. Too many companies stop training after the initial training is done. This is a systemic problem with most organizations and most leaders do not even realize that they have this issue. Your team must be committed to training on a consistent basis. This is key for culture and growth.

You do not need to be a billion-dollar company and you do not need a fancy training program to have an ongoing training program. In today's world, there is so much information and training right online. It is there for any industry that you could think of and you could take advantage of that training for your team. Continuing to train your people on a weekly or monthly basis is a commitment to the company and to their career. A company without ongoing training in today's world will not do well and will die, as things are moving very fast.

Seek out new ways to train and develop your team. It must be ongoing, and you must put the effort in to get it done.

Our newest workforce, which are millennials and Generation Z, have a different impression of training. They do not do well when they do not know what is going on and need a lot of attention. Do yourself a favor and make sure that you are consistently training your team. This training could be anything from YouTube videos to in the field training to on-the-job training. In fact, it must be all of them.

Our new generation wants quick bits of training. A 60-minute video is not going to teach anything. Short 2-3 minute how to videos are key. Break it down into little bits so your audience can digest it. I am not a millennial, well I'm right at the beginning but I will not watch an instructional video that is more than 4 minutes long, I simply cannot stand it.

You must know your audience. It's funny I have heard many people tell me that a video must be 2-3 minutes, or you lose your audience, but then they produce a 15-minute video. Talk about out of touch even with there own thoughts.

Training and support must happen on a consistent basis if you want to have a winning service team.

This last piece concludes the 5 steps of a successful customer service business. You must use all of them and it is wise to have a plan to put it all together.

There is not one part of the 5 steps that is more important than the other. They must all be done and are equality important to your success providing the best service possible and building a great customer service company.

Chapter 6
Putting it all together

As I said at the beginning of this book, there are many customer service books out there. I have tried to make his book a very concise guide that you could quickly reference if you forget what you need to do to provide good customer service. I want you to remember the five steps to building a great customer service company. This is something anyone can do if you put in the work.

Customer service is a mind set and must be part of every system in your company. You can use the ideas in this book, in any stage of your company, from those just starting out to a company that is well established. The concept is the same. Put your customers first and follow the 5 steps.

1. Hire the right people: They must want to help every customer you serve.

2. Set the rules/vision: You must make sure everyone knows exactly what you expect from them.

3. Build the culture: Service is your main objective, without your customers, you have nothing. Build the culture around the vision, the two-work hand and hand.

4. Get everyone involved: Without keeping everyone involved and up to date you will not build the customer Service Company you want.

5. Consistently train: ABT, always be training. Without training you will have a bunch of poorly trained team members.

Follow up: The last thing that puts everything together is follow up.

With all the ideas in this book and I've tried to provide a very clear, concise, message for you to follow so you can perform and maintain exceptional service.

If you do all of this, the main thing you must do after all things are set up, is to follow-up. The follow-up is very important, and you must follow-up consistently. This must be communicated in a way that you keep your team engaged.

Connectivity is a very big part of making sure this works. If you hire the right people, set the vision, build the culture, and don't get everyone trained and involved you will fail. If you do all the steps you will be on your way to building a great customer service company.

You must follow-up consistently and without follow-up, your team loses interest. They will take your lack of follow-up as you do not care and that you are not interested in them or their work. You will seem disconnected, and your team will not follow you.

Remember as much as you need to know your team, your team needs to know you as well. If they don't, you will not get the buy in that you want.

By following up, you will lead your team in such a way that they will always understand the rules and the directives of your company. With the follow-up, you will guide them through the new changes and issues that come up in any company.

Follow-up with the team should be daily and does change with different positions.

If you have a multi-location company, you might just follow-up with the managers daily and not all employees. The daily follow-up, in this case, will be left to your managers or supervisors in each location.

COVID has also changed this and made it easier to follow-up with everyone. Now we use ZOOM, Teams, and other forms of video conferencing daily. We have established a system where we can touch multiple people in different places with the stroke of a keyboard. The new way is very efficient as I can be in multiple states at once and people can see exactly what I want. This should not take away from your in-person stuff. In person is where it is at, and it must be done. As I have said many times, in this book, you must keep the connectivity with your people, or they will feel as if you do not care. There is nothing like working in the trenches with a teammate; that is what makes great service.

If you are one of those managers or supervisors in an individual location, you must follow-up and communicate with your team daily. Everyone from the newest employee to the oldest employee needs your attention. They also need your daily follow-up and your direction no matter how good they are.

Using these 5 steps will provide for a wonderful experience for both your team and your customers.

My hope, for you, is that you truly embrace customer service for both yourself and for your team. It is a very powerful thing to build a wonderful service business and, if you are committed to it, you can do it.

Customer service truly must be the main thing that you and your company stands for. You must make sure everyone employed, in your company, believes and stands for doing the right thing for each customer, always. If you do not have this, you will not be able to build a great customer service company.

The best thing about customer service is no one can ever question or make excuses for not providing it. Someone can make excuses for not selling enough or producing enough, but you cannot make excuses for not treating a customer correctly. It's just non-negotiable.

Therefore, to summarize, to build a great customer Service Company, you must, hire the right people, continuously trying to develop, set rules, build the culture to involve everyone, train continuously and then follow-up.

If you do these things, I guarantee that you will not only build a strong team you will be on your way to building a great customer service company.

Bonus Chapter
Thoughts on general work attitude

These are very important in everything you do.

1. Attitude
2. Willingness to complete projects
3. Timing
4. Vision
5. Demeanor

I worked my way up in a fortune 500 company from the bottom at very young age. I do not think I am smarter than the average bear; I just have the attitude and will to get any job done.
Through the years I thankfully had the support of my family to guide me through the ins and outs of working for a company and making the most of every opportunity.

The reason some people are successful, and some people are not (whether employed or self-employed) boils down to the 5 things at the beginning of this chapter. We will go over all 5 and my opinions on them in this chapter.

As I said before I am not saying I'm smarter than the average bear or that my opinions are gospel, but this is the way I see it and hopefully my advice serves you well.

1. Attitude:

Whether they were raised with the attitude or became disgruntled at some point. The common denominator I have seen in unsuccessful people is a poor or negative attitude.

On the other of this coin are successful people having the reverse, they have a positive attitude. I'm saying you can have a great attitude and money will fall from the sky, NO! But I can promise a lot more opportunity if you have a can-do attitude. The first thing a manager or boss picks up on is your attitude and if you portray everything, she/he asks you to do as a problem they will pick up on this and label you as the problem.

Let me give you an example. Your employer gives you a task to do that you really dislike. You can do three things, not do it, and quit, be upset and do it anyway, or accept the fact that she/he pays you to work and do the job the best you can. Now the first one will have you looking for a new job, the second one will get the task done but ruin your day and possibly some of the company's customer's days.

The third option will get the job done, you'll get paid, and your employer and customer will be happy.

As a matter of fact, if it's a particularly tedious task you will most likely be held in high regard by your employer for getting it done with a great attitude.

The third one is the best choice, but it is also a choice that requires rational thought and a positive can-do attitude.
Ask yourself, what would you do in the above situation? If you answered 1 or 2, you know you need to check your attitude. If it was the second one, most likely your manager, if they are any good will pick up on the negativity and remember it. There are people out there that are not smarter than you but will do the job that you have, with a smile on their face and that is what your manager is looking for.

Up until a few years ago I did not think you could train or teach attitude adjusting but since then I have proved that it works.
The only caveat to training for a good attitude is the participant must be willing to change. This requires you to not only believe that you and your job are important, but it requires you to respect the job you are currently doing as the best job for you currently.
Attitude is up to you and only you can make that choice.

2. Willingness to complete projects and be on time:

The second thing that can make or break your career is how you do your job. When you complete a task, it should be complete and on time.
It sounds simple but in a work environment if you consistently strive to be thorough you will stand out from the rest of the work force. Remember in school if you did not turn in an assignment on time it was a zero, so how does it happen in the work world?

In the bosses' mind or in your customers mind if you are self-employed every zero adds up and at the end of the day you will either be fired, or you will lose your customers. In the work force we get graded on what we deliverer.
Nothing should be missing, no mistakes, double and triple checked. No matter what the job no one should have to come to you and say you turned this in, and x and y were not done. Careless mistakes should not happen and if you check your work several times they will not. If something is due Monday, your manager/customer should have it Monday complete and ready for the next step.

Making sure a project is complete even at the most trivial level shows your employee or customer you really care about what you do. This leads to further opportunity and more money to save!

The reverse is true if something is late or not complete.

Your manager or customer will think you do not care, and you will not be looked at for promotion or additional business. This includes any small mistake including grammar, punctuation, and sentence structure in emails. You must be precise in everything you do.

3. Timing

Timing is a funny thing that is often looked at and confused with luck. Timing is not luck it's the insight that time is correct now to do something. If you have a great attitude and you have the willingness to complete projects on time your timing will fall into place. Let me give your simple example. You're going to cross a street; you see cars coming so you see that the car is going slow enough that you can cross. You move and cross the street.

Was that luck? No, it was timing! The same is true in your career. Timing is basically logic-based hope that something will work in your favor.
In business it is not as easy as crossing the street, but the same principles work. If you work harder than the next person in your same position you will get noticed and you will move up. The person that works the hardest and makes sure he/she is open to any work will get the bosses or customers attention.

4. Vision

Your vision for yourself is one of the most important things. If you do not know where you want to go you cannot expect you will get there. To clarify you need to have a vision or plan for what and where your life is going to end up.
As I stated previously in this book you must have a plan. This can include everything from your work to your personal goals. You must not only have these goals but vocalize them, so you are expected to achieve them. Make sure you have a vision of what and where you want to be, both financially as well as personally.

5. *Demeanor:*

Your demeanor is how people see you and how you interact with others. You can be the smartest person in the room but if you have a poor demeanor.

When this is the case you will not be recognized, and you will not advance in your career or anything you do. On the other hand, if you have a great demeanor you will attract attention and set yourself up to have many opportunities in your professional and personal life.

These five things I have gone through will ensure your success in whatever you do as a career. Although it is easier said than done this is something you should work at and will surely make you more successful in your life.

Thank you for purchasing my book. My goal is to get this into the hands of as many people as possible. If you like the book, please share it with your peers. If you ever have any questions I love to hear from my readers and can be contacted on LinkedIn. I wish you luck in building a great customer service company.

Remember to your employees and customers, YOUR CUSTOMER SERVICE MATTERS.

www.ingramcontent.com/pod-product-compliance
Lightning Source LLC
LaVergne TN
LVHW051703080426
835511LV00017B/2707